I WANT TO BE A
SEA CAPTAIN

Written by
Jonathan Reule

Illustration
Caballero Peza Mauricio
&
Caballero Peza Gabriel Fernando

Storyboard
Chong Wey Ming & Christiane Tee

UNIBINO

B O O K S

First paperback edition October 2023
ISBN 978-981-18-7876-3

Published by Unibino Pte. Ltd.
9 North Buona Vista Drive, #02-01 Metropolis Tower 1, Singapore 138588

www.unibino.com

Water is a major source of life on our planet. Without this simple yet dynamic compound, life would cease to exist. From our earliest days of mankind, we have been naturally drawn to these bodies of water as a source of comfort and, ultimately, a source of life.

Thankfully we are lucky in the grand scheme of the universe that over 71 per cent of our planet's surface is covered in water. Giving us many plentiful sources of water for our survival. However, having so many bodies of water surrounding us also leaves us with several obstacles to navigate.

This is why having boats and other watercraft are essential in our modern world. You see, these water vessels can help us traverse the many watery obstacles in our way. From smaller boats helping us to cross large rivers to giant cargo freighters crossing the oceans, these vessels have become fundamental modes of transport on this planet.

But what good are these maritime vessels without anyone to captain them? If someone asked you to steer a massive cargo ship today, could you handle it? Even if you might be able to control it, would you be able to navigate such a ship across the Atlantic Ocean to its port of call? If you're like most of us, then you probably won't be able to, which is why we need skilled captains in our modern world to keep our many ships and sea vessels afloat!

Before sailing any further, it's good for us to reverse and look at maritime history to understand the foundations of this noble profession. As mentioned earlier, water covers the majority of our planet, making it necessary for us to figure out a way to travel over these bodies of water.

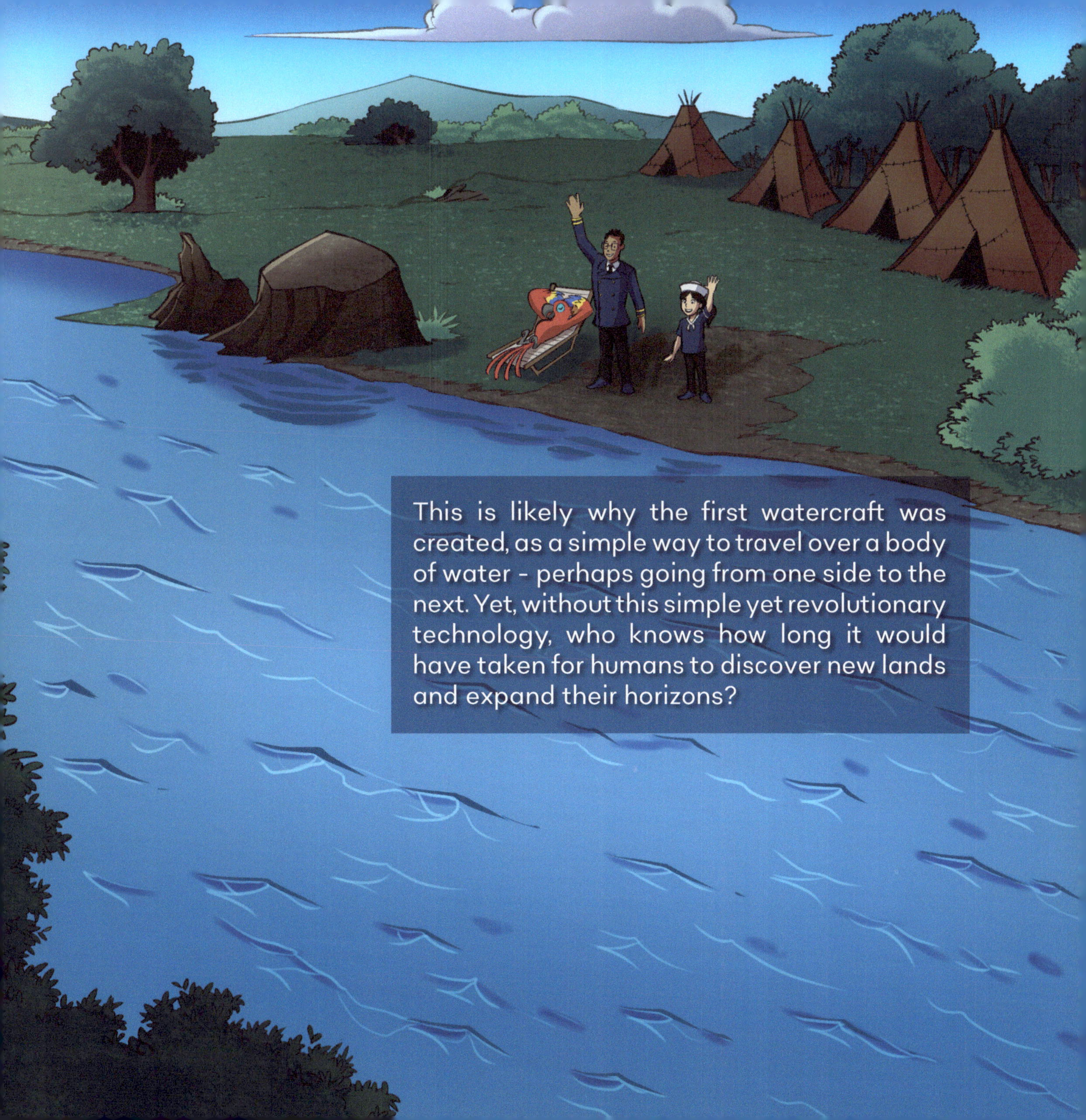

This is likely why the first watercraft was created, as a simple way to travel over a body of water - perhaps going from one side to the next. Yet, without this simple yet revolutionary technology, who knows how long it would have taken for humans to discover new lands and expand their horizons?

And that's exactly what many civilisations did. They began exploring beyond their terrestrial boundaries by making basic watercrafts which they could use to explore the giant lakes and seas between them and their neighbours. Take the Beaker culture in the prehistoric UK as an example.

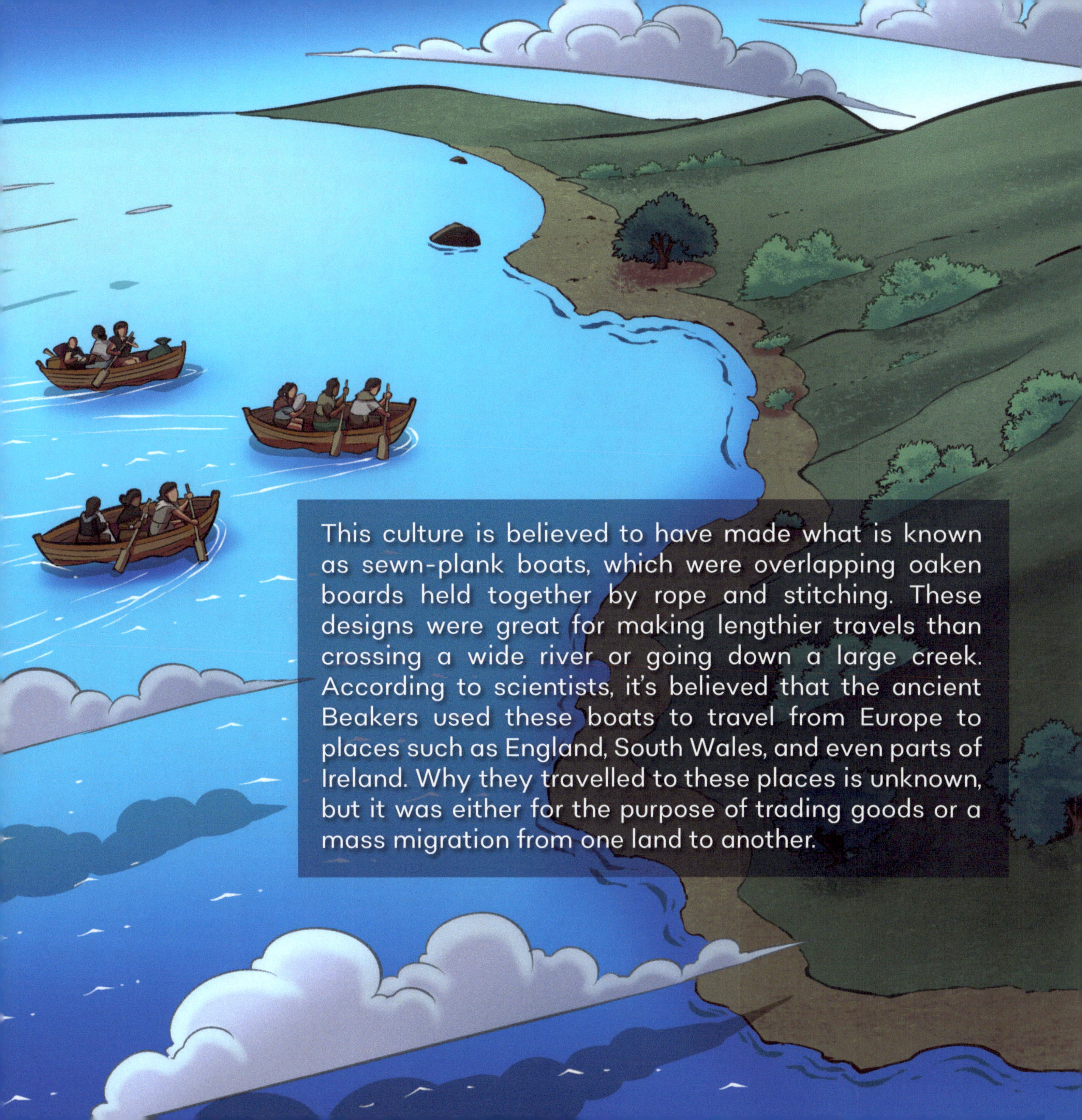

This culture is believed to have made what is known as sewn-plank boats, which were overlapping oaken boards held together by rope and stitching. These designs were great for making lengthier travels than crossing a wide river or going down a large creek. According to scientists, it's believed that the ancient Beakers used these boats to travel from Europe to places such as England, South Wales, and even parts of Ireland. Why they travelled to these places is unknown, but it was either for the purpose of trading goods or a mass migration from one land to another.

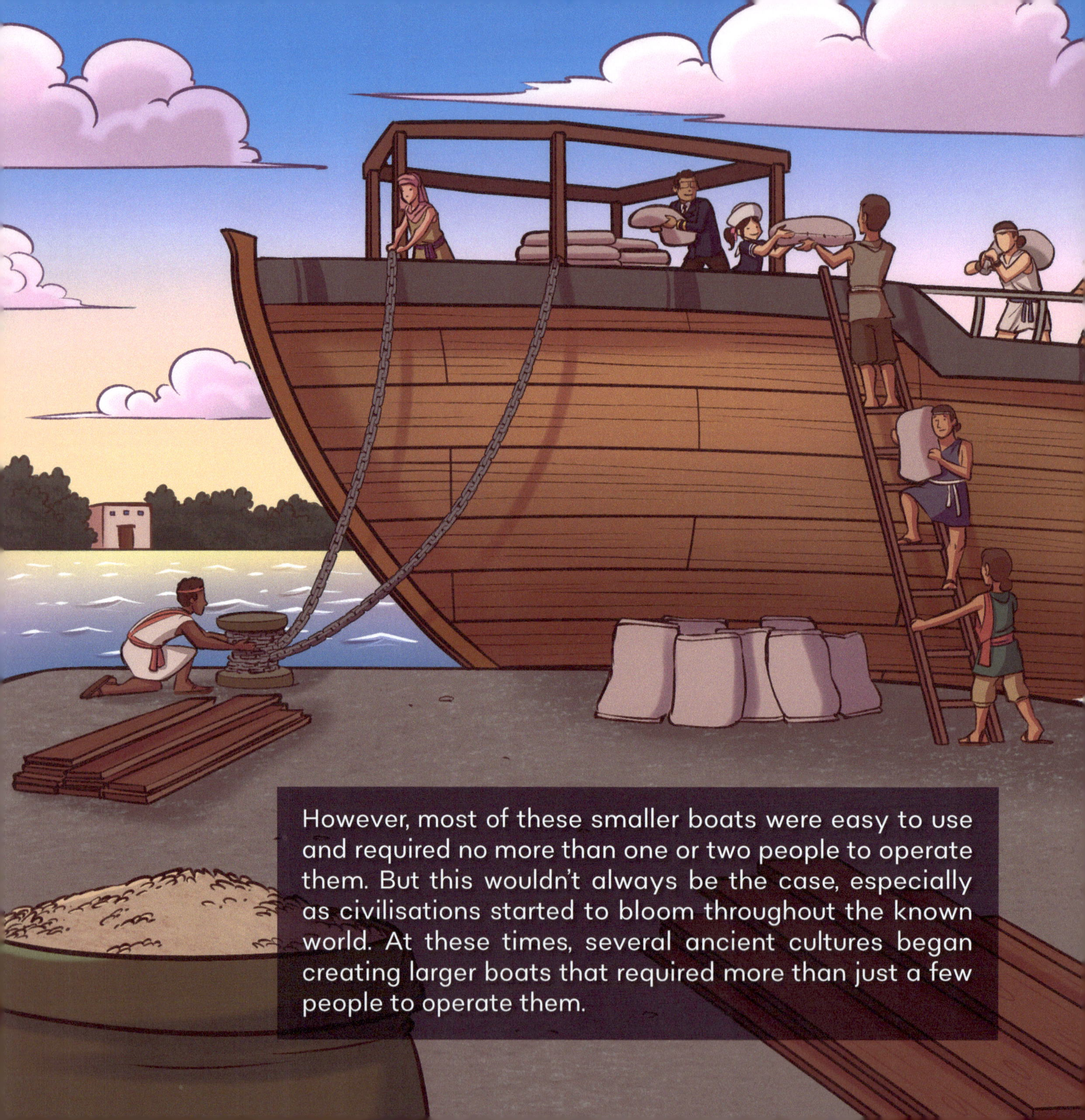

However, most of these smaller boats were easy to use and required no more than one or two people to operate them. But this wouldn't always be the case, especially as civilisations started to bloom throughout the known world. At these times, several ancient cultures began creating larger boats that required more than just a few people to operate them.

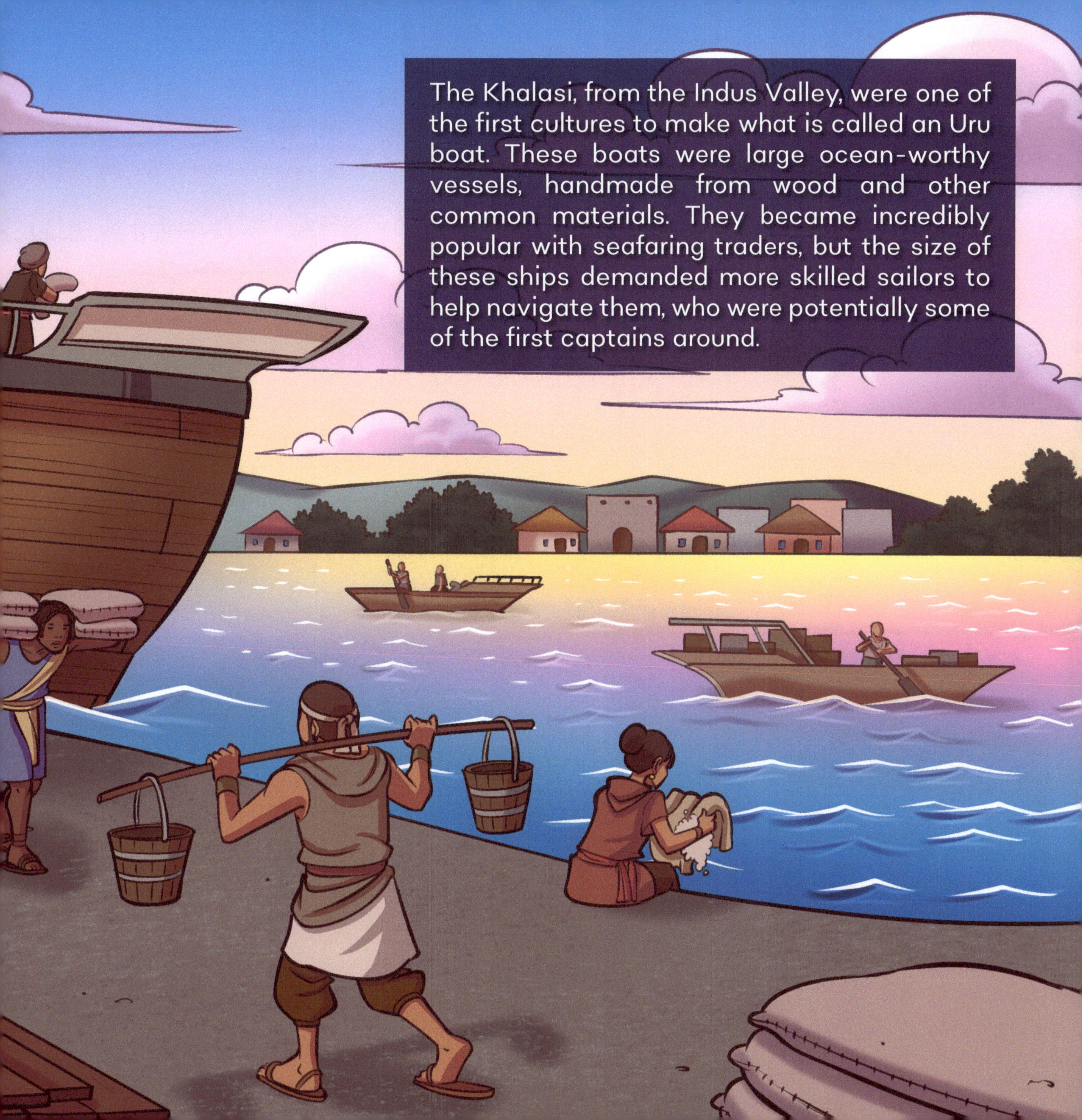
The Khalasi, from the Indus Valley, were one of the first cultures to make what is called an Uru boat. These boats were large ocean-worthy vessels, handmade from wood and other common materials. They became incredibly popular with seafaring traders, but the size of these ships demanded more skilled sailors to help navigate them, who were potentially some of the first captains around.

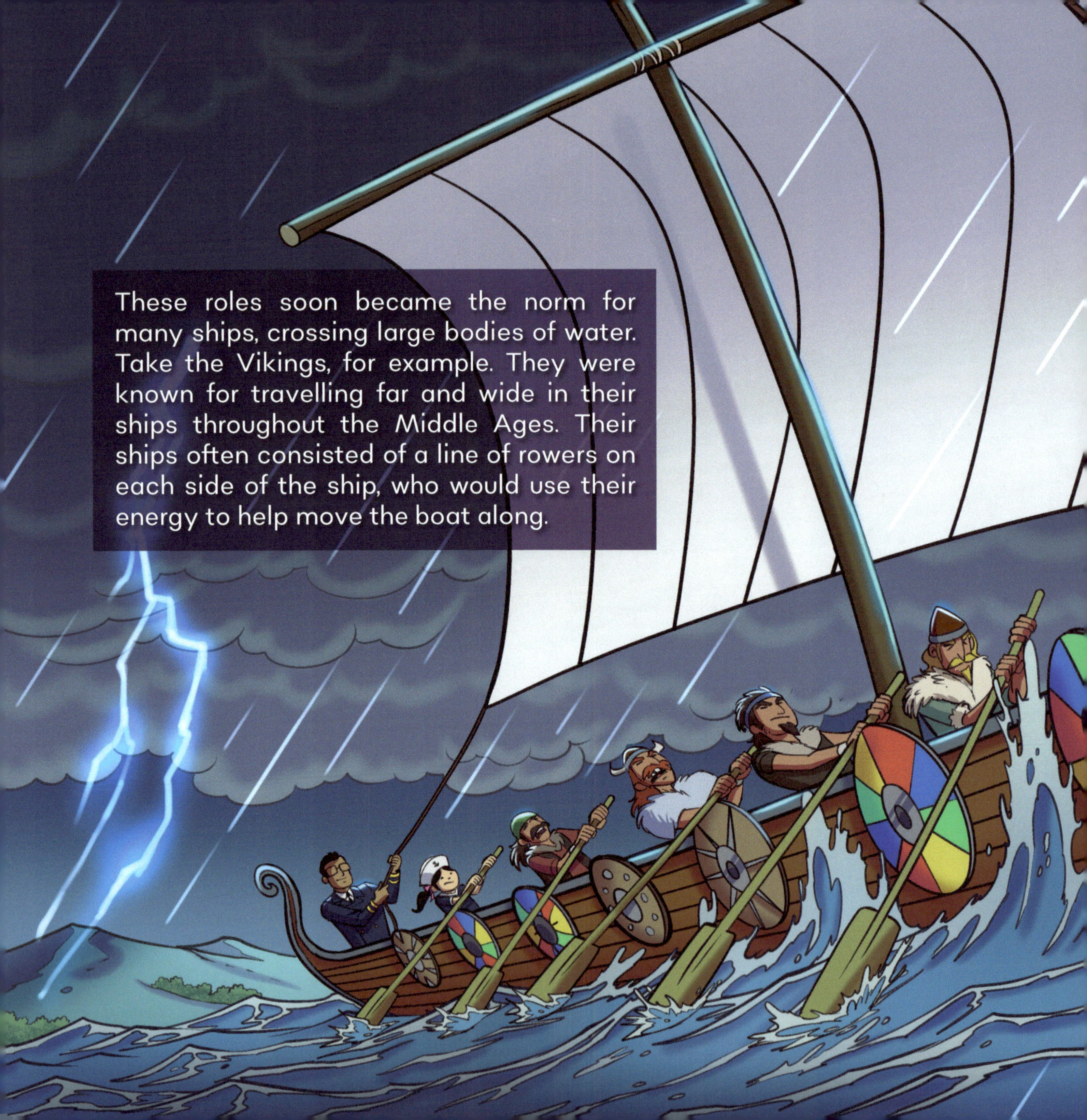

These roles soon became the norm for many ships, crossing large bodies of water. Take the Vikings, for example. They were known for travelling far and wide in their ships throughout the Middle Ages. Their ships often consisted of a line of rowers on each side of the ship, who would use their energy to help move the boat along.

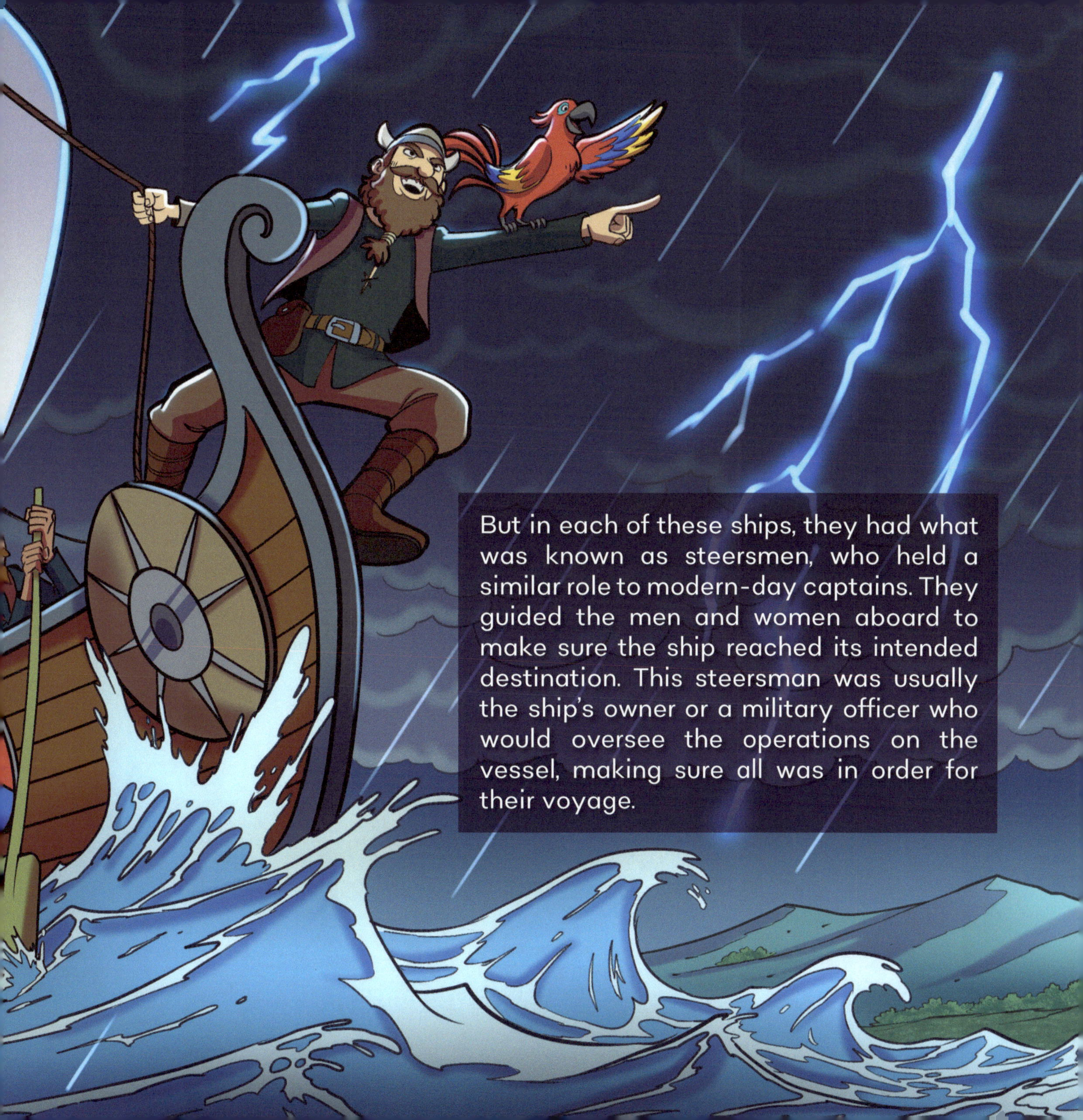

But in each of these ships, they had what was known as steersmen, who held a similar role to modern-day captains. They guided the men and women aboard to make sure the ship reached its intended destination. This steersman was usually the ship's owner or a military officer who would oversee the operations on the vessel, making sure all was in order for their voyage.

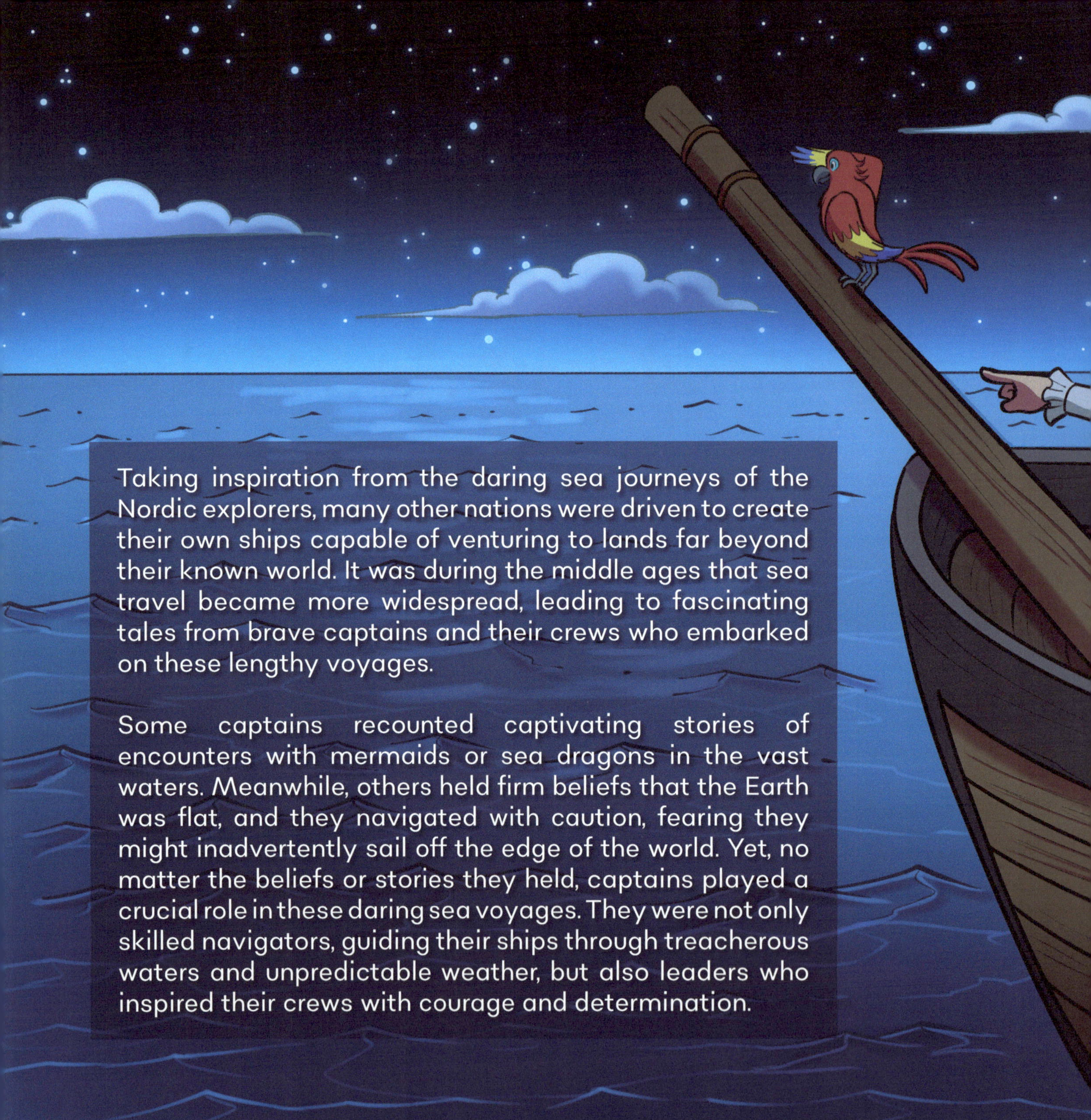

Taking inspiration from the daring sea journeys of the Nordic explorers, many other nations were driven to create their own ships capable of venturing to lands far beyond their known world. It was during the middle ages that sea travel became more widespread, leading to fascinating tales from brave captains and their crews who embarked on these lengthy voyages.

Some captains recounted captivating stories of encounters with mermaids or sea dragons in the vast waters. Meanwhile, others held firm beliefs that the Earth was flat, and they navigated with caution, fearing they might inadvertently sail off the edge of the world. Yet, no matter the beliefs or stories they held, captains played a crucial role in these daring sea voyages. They were not only skilled navigators, guiding their ships through treacherous waters and unpredictable weather, but also leaders who inspired their crews with courage and determination.

And as these ships grew larger, the role of a captain became all the more important. In the Renaissance, advancements in shipbuilding techniques allowed the construction of grand vessels that dwarfed their predecessors from the Middle Ages. These majestic ships, known as galleons and carracks, possessed towering masts and vast hulls capable of carrying substantial cargo and numerous crew members.

The increase in ship size presented new challenges and required skilled captains to navigate these immense vessels effectively. Captains had to possess a deep understanding of the ship's dimensions, weight distribution, and manoeuvring capabilities. They skillfully directed the crew in hoisting and adjusting the colossal sails, harnessing the power of the wind to propel the ship forward with remarkable speed and efficiency.

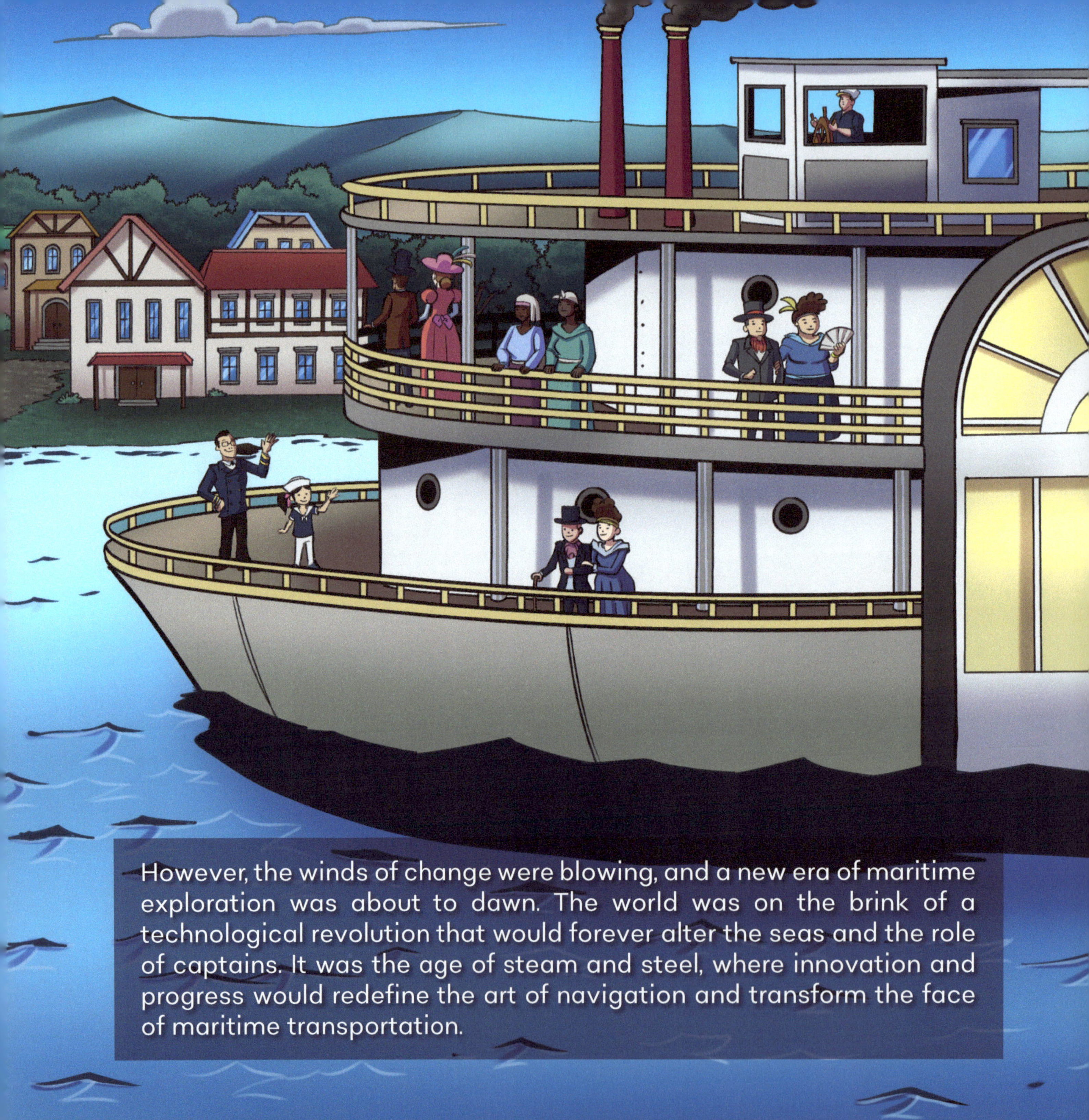
However, the winds of change were blowing, and a new era of maritime exploration was about to dawn. The world was on the brink of a technological revolution that would forever alter the seas and the role of captains. It was the age of steam and steel, where innovation and progress would redefine the art of navigation and transform the face of maritime transportation.

The advent of steam-powered ships brought about a radical shift in the captain's responsibilities and the dynamics of seafaring. No longer solely reliant on the whims of the wind, these steamships could propel themselves forward using the power of steam engines. This meant that captains now had to master the operation and maintenance of complex machinery, understanding the complexities of steam engines, boilers, and propellers.

This, of course, brings us to modern-day maritime operations, where Captains play a key role in ensuring the safe and timely passage of their ships. But learning all of this may have you wondering what it takes to become a ship's captain in today's world. Well, first, it's important to understand what is required of a ship's captain and how it will impact your life.

One thing you'll need to prepare for is the amount of time you'll spend out at sea, as most shipping lanes can take a boat a month or more to transit. That means you could be away from land, family, and friends for sometimes up to 60 days in one go! So, a ship's captain needs to be mentally, physically, and emotionally prepared to endure a long journey out at sea.

Another thing ship captains will need is a strong mathematical foundation and a deep understanding of mechanical engineering. These are important for a ship's captain to know so that they can properly navigate to and from their intended destinations and have a good understanding of the ship's mechanics. That's why most ship captains have a bachelor's degree in a related field of either Marine Science or Engineering.

But these ship captains should also have another key attribute that can sometimes be overlooked - they should be comfortable in a leadership role. Being the highest ranking officer on a ship, they may be forced to make hard decisions while others are worried and concerned. And it wouldn't help to calm any of the crewmembers aboard if the captain got shakey at every problematic situation that arises!

Next, it's good to know what type of captain you'd like to be. For starters, there is always a need for Port Captains, who are often located on the shore, working to ensure that all the vessels coming and leaving port are up to international safety standards before sailing.

Among those ships inspected are often Cargo Ships, which make up the majority of non-military vessels in our modern world. Having so many things to ship to and from different countries has created a big demand for Cargo Ship Captains to commandeer these vessels. They make sure all cargo is stowed safely and reaches its destination in good shape (instead of ending up at the bottom of the sea!)

Another popular occupation in the maritime field is Fishing Vessel Captain. As you can probably tell from the name, this type of captain takes charge of large fishing vessels, often taking them to hot spots in the ocean that are plentiful with fish! The captain may also need to navigate their vessel to dangerous areas, such as the artic, where the waves can be extremely choppy, and the weather is below freezing! In this case, the captain should be well-experienced before taking on such a tricky mission!

Whereas a Cruise Ship Captain is a revered leader responsible for navigating and managing large cruise liners, ensuring smooth voyages and unforgettable experiences for passengers. They possess extensive knowledge of maritime navigation, safety protocols, and vessel handling. In addition to their operational duties, they act as ambassadors, maintaining positive relationships with port authorities and local communities. With their unwavering commitment and astute leadership, Cruise Ship Captains bring dreams to life and create extraordinary journeys at sea.

Fleet Captains hold a prominent role in the maritime domain, overseeing a collection of ships within a fleet. Their responsibilities encompass strategic planning, coordination, and operational management of multiple vessels. They possess a comprehensive understanding of fleet logistics, deployment strategies, and resource allocation. Fleet Captains ensure seamless communication and synchronisation among ships under their command, maximising efficiency and effectiveness.

Lastly, Ferry Captains command vessels that transport passengers and vehicles across waterways. These skilled captains navigate busy water routes, ensuring the safe and efficient transport of people and goods. They possess expert knowledge of local water conditions, including tides, currents, and navigational hazards. Ferry Captains maintain strict adherence to schedules, providing reliable transportation services to communities and travellers.

As you set your sight on the vast open seas, you'll discover that each ship holds its own secrets and challenges. But under the expert guidance of a seasoned Ship Captain, these maritime marvels become a realm of adventure and wonder for all aboard.

Now, young mariner, the decision lies with you. Will you dare to embark on the path of a Ship Captain, destined to chart new courses and lead your crew through uncharted waters? The tides of history await your command! So, get out there and make your dreams a reality!

Shubhi Saxena
Founder, Unibino

My Inspiration

As a parent in this ever-changing world, it can sometimes feel overwhelming when it comes to our children's futures. New technologies seem to be arising almost every day, and with so many innovations, it creates unique professions which many of us wouldn't have dreamed to be necessary only a few years ago. Which to me is a good thing. Because with so much variety, my children can have the opportunity to pick a career that will fit their personalities and build upon their strengths. As you may imagine, this desire within me to provide my children with the resources they needed to thrive, led me to search out books that would be easy enough for them to understand while teaching them about various professions.

Only, I found that these books were few and far between. Even if I could find a book about a certain profession geared towards young readers, I found them sparse inside and limited to only certain careers that may not fit my children's abilities. This is when I came up with the idea to write my own children's books, teaching them about all the various careers in the modern world. After months of researching different professions and learning more than I ever expected, I quickly realised this was going to be a bigger project than I first anticipated. I dove into the histories of these professions, discovering links to the past, and why these professions were now so important.

Ultimately my goal was to offer my children options, to show them that there is no one set path for everyone. But in this, I stumbled upon something bigger. I wanted to share this with future generations. To share with all children and parents about these careers, to help spark curiosity, and to instil a passion for the future. Everyone has special talents and abilities, and I hope that this series will be able to offer clarity and inspiration to children around the world. Because at the end of the day, it's never too early to start dreaming and never too late to take action. With this, I hope you enjoy this series and that your young ones become the best versions of themselves as they can achieve.